Therefore go and make disciples of all nations, baptizing them in the name of the Father and of the Son and of the Holy Spirit, 20 and teaching them to obey everything I have commanded you. And surely I am with you always, to the very end of the age.

Matthew 28:19-20 (NIV)

EXPANDING THE EXPEDITION through DIGITAL MINISTRY

Nicole Reilley

EXPANDING THE EXPEDITION THROUGH DIGITAL MINISTRY

books@marketsquarebooks.com
141 N. Martinwood Rd. Knoxville TN 37923
ISBN: 978-1-950899-38-8

Printed and Bound in the United States of America

Contributing Editor: Kay Kotan

Unless noted, Scripture quotations taken from the following version of the Holy Bible:

NIV

This resource was commissioned as one of many interconnected steps in the journey of *The Greatest Expedition*.

GreatestExpedition.com

Table of Contents

Foreword

This resource was commissioned as one of many interconnected steps in the journey of *The Greatest Expedition.* While each step is important individually, we intentionally built the multi-step Essentials Pack and the Expansion Pack to provide a richer and fuller experience with the greatest potential for transformation and introducing more people to a relationship with Jesus Christ. For more information, visit GreatestExpedition.org.

However, we also recognize you may be exploring this resource apart from *The Greatest Expedition.* You might find yourself on a personal journey, a small group journey, or perhaps a church leadership team journey. We are so glad you are on this journey!

As you take each step in your expedition, your Expedition Team will discover whether the ministry tools you will be exploring will be utilized only for the Expedition Team or if this expedition will be a congregational journey. Our hope and prayer is *The Greatest Expedition* is indeed a congregational journey, but if it proves to be a solo journey for just the Expedition Team, God will still do amazing things through your intentional exploration, discernment, and faithful next steps.

Regardless of how you came to discover *The Greatest Expedition,* it will pave the way to a new God-inspired expedition. Be brave and courageous on your journey through *The Greatest Expedition!*

Kay L Kotan, PCC
Director, *The Greatest Expedition*

INTRODUCTION
Welcome to the Digital Edition!

We're about to take seriously the world in which we find ourselves. We live in a digital world, and regardless of your age (you may or may not be a digital native) or comfort with technology, all of us find ourselves living in a time when God is using technology to build up the church.

This expedition doesn't require any unique skill set, only a desire to let God lead as we use today's tools for God's glory. Don't let the topic scare you if this is new to you. We will make it accessible and fun. And remember, everything on our expedition is a process, a discovery, an unfolding of where God is calling us as his church.

This book is part of *The Greatest Expedition*

Expansion Pack.[1] If you've been participating in an expedition team, you have some excellent skills already, and I trust your confidence will grow as you learn about how you can use digital media to reach new people, connect with your current community and share the Gospel. If you are not part of an expedition team, you will find this resource will connect you and your church to our digital present.

First, a word about our title. We're joining in a digital expedition, not a virtual expedition. The term "virtual" is often used when we talk about the Web, online communities (like Facebook), and the connections and relationships we form. But there is a problem with the word *virtual*. It connotes connections that are "almost" or second best.

But let me be clear, we will not be making the case that online relationships and connections are the same as in-person ones; we all know they are not. But we will be talking about why online connections are valuable, and there is nothing "virtual" or "almost" about them.

As someone who is not a digital native (that

---

1 Greatestexpedition.com

is, someone who grew up always having access to the Web), I am a digital immigrant. I never thought that online connections could be one essential way I connected, practiced spiritual disciplines, and led others to grow as a disciple. But that is what happened to me. Over the last five years, my most significant spiritual growth came about because I was in an ongoing small group that meets via Zoom. From all around the country, this group of five came together when I taught an online discipleship class. We enjoyed each other so much that most of us have been able to stay together and have grown into a close-knit community, sharing life's ups and downs as we listen to where God is leading. Of the five, only three of us had met in person, and so our relationships were digital-first, in-person second as we worked to meet up.

Your experience may be different, but regardless of your experience with online communities, the digital world is here, and we have an opportunity, one we are just starting to take hold of, for the Church and the Gospel.

Tom Rainer, in his book, *The Post-Quarantine Church: Six Urgent Challenges and Opportunities That Will Determine the Future of Your Congregation,*[2] writes that there are at least three ways people use technology in relation to the church.

1. **Digital-only** – "People who are physically unable to attend in-person gatherings. They could be anyone from elderly shut-ins to members of the armed forces stationed overseas."

2. **Digitally transitioning** – "They are still mostly connected to the church digitally. They rarely, if ever, attend an in-person gathering. But there are indications they are somewhat open to connecting in person. Perhaps they've joined a video-based small group and have begun to get to know others better..."

3. **Dual Citizens** – "They are connected to your congregation both digitally and in person. This distinction is important to remember. It's pretty rare anymore to find someone who has no digital connections, even if they strongly prefer in-person gatherings."

Many of us are Dual Citizens, but during COVID, many of us found ourselves becoming Digital Only. In today's world, we will be seeing

---

[2] Rainer, Thom S. (2020) *The Post-Quarantine Church: Six Urgent Challenges and Opportunities That Will Determine the Future of Your Congregation,* Tyndale Momentum, Page 31.

people make a variety of choices on how they connect to the church. Because of that, offering both in-person and digital experiences enables us to engage more fully in the mission God has put before us.

This resource will look at why the digital world matters to God, the distinctions between online worship and online ministry, the differences between our approaches to ministry online and in-person, evangelism, engagement and why it matters, and hybrid ministry models.

So, let's begin.

CHAPTER ONE

Starting with Why

Let's start with the obvious: Why bother the digital world when we talk about the church? Isn't the digital world a sorry substitute for in-person gatherings? Shouldn't we want people to turn off their screens, put down their phones, and come to church to worship?

Maybe. But what if the Internet is the tool God is using to reach new people? What if the Web is keeping people connected in times when they cannot gather in person? What if the Spirit is calling us in new directions as we hear of in Isaiah?

> *See, I am doing a new thing! Now it springs up; do you not perceive it? I am making a way in the wilderness and streams in the wasteland.*[3]

---

3 Isaiah 43:19 (NIV).

Let's consider the new before us and why we might want to go on a digital expedition by looking at the realities and the opportunities.

Reality One: It is Where the People Are

People are already connecting online. This is our first reason for going on a digital expedition.

As we touched on in the introduction, church researcher Thom Rainer describes people in various categories based on their use of technology. To review, some people are 'digital only,' never connecting outside the screen. Some people are 'digitally transitioning.' These are those who mostly connect online while also connecting to people through small groups, some of which may happen in person. And many people are 'dual citizens,' connecting in person and online. In today's world, most people use technology in some way.[4]

For example, in 2019, 90 percent of US adults reported using the Internet: 312.32

---

[4] Rainer, Thom S. (2020) *The Post-Quarantine Church: Six Urgent Challenges and Opportunities That Will Determine the Future of Your Congregation,* Tyndale Momentum. Page 31-32.

million users. By 2025, the projected number of Facebook users in the US is expected to reach 235.15 million. That is a lot of people!

So, if people's use of technology is a given, the question then becomes: Do they use it to connect to their faith, grow in their understanding of Jesus, or find a community in which to belong? Yes, evidence shows they do.

People are using the Internet to learn about faith, to find God, and to worship. A Pew Research Study from 2004 speculated that 64 percent of Americans use the Internet for "faith-related reasons."[5] While a more recent study from Baylor University puts the number lower at 45 percent,[6] studies show people use the Internet to connect to faith.

Here are some other helpful insights:

- 25 percent of Internet users have gotten religious or spiritual information online at one point or another. This is an increase from survey findings in late 2000, which showed that this continues to grow.

---

5 https://www.pewresearch.org/Internet/2004/04/07/64-of-online-americans-have-used-the-internet-for-religious-or-spiritual-purposes/.

6 https://www.baylor.edu/baylorreligionsurvey/doc.php/292546.pdf.

- 21 percent of Internet users – or between 19 million and 20 million people – have gone online to get religious or spiritual material.
- More than 3 million people a day get religious or spiritual material, up from the 2 million we reported last year.[7]

"For comparison's sake, it is interesting to note that more people have gotten religious or spiritual information online than have gambled online. More have gotten religious or spiritual information than having used Web auction sites, traded stocks online, placed phone calls on the Internet, done online banking, or used Internet-based dating services."[8] That information calls us as the Church to respond.

The statistics will change (and hopefully, more attention will be paid to tracking faith data). Still, technology isn't going away, and its use, especially by younger people, will continue to expand.

---

7 https://www.pewresearch.org/Internet/2001/12/23/cyber-faith-how-americans-pursue-religion-online/#how-americans-pursue-religion-online.

8 Ibid.

"Overall, about four out of every five Americans own a smartphone. However, for those under 45 years old, smartphone ownership is ubiquitous – roughly 94 percent of 18 to 44-year-olds own smartphones. For Americans 65 and older, over half own a smartphone. Meanwhile, most Americans also stay connected through social media on social networking sites like Facebook, Twitter, or Instagram. Seven out of 10 Americans have a social networking profile, with 96 percent of 18-24-year-olds reporting to have one."[9]

The use of apps to study the Bible or connect to their local congregation's Web-based offerings (including online giving) offers a growing opportunity for any faith community to connect with current congregational members and seekers.

Why connect digitally? Because a simple rule of church growth is "go where the numbers are," and the numbers are on the Web. Think of it this way – would you instead go fishing in a pond where the fish are few or a pond where the fish are plentiful and hungry for the worm on your hook?

---

9 https://www.baylor.edu/baylorreligionsurvey/doc.php/292546.pdf page 50.

Reality Two: The Ongoing Decline of In-Person Attendance:

The second reason to go on this digital expedition is there continues to be a growing decline of in-person attendance and growth of the 'nones.' That is, those with no religious affiliation.[10]

Most of us have experienced the decline of in-person worship attendance. Is connecting digitally one way to address this reality?

In 2016, the Pew Research Center found that people who report going to church less now than they used to say that the logistics of getting there is one deterrent.[11] Others attend worship less often due to the reality that a full one-third of working adults has work responsibilities on Sunday morning.[12]

No longer are businesses closed on weekends, and the complexities of balancing

---

[10] https://www.pewresearch.org/fact-tank/2018/08/08/why-americas-nones-dont-identify-with-a-religion/.

[11] https://www.pewforum.org/2016/08/23/2-religious-attendance-fluid-for-many-americans/.

[12] From US Bureau of Labor Statistics, "American time us survey – m2018 Results" news release no USDL-19-1003 June 19, 2019m https://www.bls.gov/news.release/pdf/atus.pdf.

kids and work can make Sunday at 10 AM a problematic hour to attend. This is especially true with the young. For while Protestant statistics were less available, one would imagine the statistic that only 15 percent of young adult Catholics attend worship weekly, while 72 percent are using social networks, which isn't too different from the average mainline church experience.

The rise of the "nones" is well documented at 21 percent of the population. A Pew Research Center study reports that in addition to that 21 percent, an additional 16 percent identify as "neither spiritual nor religious."[13] Who are these people?

"Two-thirds of them say they believe in God (68 percent). More than half say they often feel a deep connection with nature and the earth (58 percent), while more than a third classify themselves as "spiritual" but not "religious" (37 percent), and one-in-five (21 percent) say they pray every day..."[14]

---

[13] Berger, Teresa (2017) @ *Worship: Liturgical Practices in Digital Worlds* (Liturgy, Worship and Society Series) Routledge, Kindle Edition, Page 3.

[14] https://www.pewforum.org/2012/10/09/nones-on-the-rise/.

It is no secret that most churches have older members and have struggled to attract younger and more ethnically diverse members. Old models of just doing what we have always done but adding drums or screens aren't changing the realities many churches face: many churches sit emptier every year.

"The signs of the times are thus quite clear: the digital age and digitally suffused living are here. And it would be nonsensical to assume that practices of worship and prayer are the one area of life immune to and untouched by the advent of the digital age."[15]

We must connect digitally because the people are online, and reaching them with in-person offerings has become more complicated and will become even harder each passing year.

But just because people are online and fewer come to our church building, does it mean my local church should spend time, energy, and money pursuing a digital presence?

---

[15] Berger, Teresa (2017) @ *Worship: Liturgical Practices in Digital Worlds* (Liturgy, Worship and Society Series) Routledge, Kindle Edition, page 3.

Some would say no. There will be people who decline to go on a digital expedition for a variety of good reasons. Scott McKnight, in the Foreword to *Analogue Church,* writes,

> *"One can't 'do' church digitally; the important things about church life are all embodied: knowing one another, loving one another, sitting and standing and praying with one another, listening to the sermon and watching the tone of the words and the movement of the body when we sing and walk forward to take communion. These are the things that make a church a church."*[16]

I agree with Scott, and yet I also think a digital expedition is something churches are called to embrace. As I have explored the various types of church models, I wonder if online ministry is just one expression of church, no more faithful or less faithful than a mid-size church or a rural family size church is.

The Church has always had a variety of expressions. Some churches are house churches. Others are small family-size churches, mid-size program churches,

---

[16] Kim, Jay Y (2020) *Analogue Church: Why We Need Real People, Place and Things in the Digital Age,* IVP, Kindle Edition, Forward by Scot McKnight, Page 2.

megachurches, or cathedrals, but each can be a faithful expression of what God calls the church to be. Can a digital ministry be just one more expression?

Yes, I believe it can. Whether that is a digital expression of a brick-and-mortar church or a totally online ministry, a digital expedition opens doors to reach new people and connect with existing groups. You and I may have our preferences for church size or style of worship and ministry, but that preference doesn't make one type invalid. Instead, the diversity of sizes and styles leads to opportunity – we can reach more – new and more diverse – people.

As we consider and explore digital ministry, we may need to consider some mindset shifts to embrace this emerging ministry approach. Let's investigate some shifts together.

Mindset Shift: Thinking through Quality of Presence

Before we can embrace this for our local contexts, I think we have to spend some time talking about the most significant difference between online and in-person ministry – the quality of presence.

Quality of presence refers to the genuine differences between how we are present when we are physically in a building and present online.

Are we present to one another in an authentic way when we're on a digital expedition?

Douglas Estes, author of *Simchurch,* writes of our very real struggle to define church and how "being present" is a big part of what being a church has meant.[17] Digital expressions of worship, discipleship, and small groups are often thought to be less than in-person experiences. But Estes reflects that as we become more comfortable with technology, this may be changing.

We have tended to think of church as a physical space where people gather together. We tend to think of a congregation as those who gather in a church building. Yet, a digital expedition challenges this. Can we authentically be a church congregation online?

We have seen some ask this question in light of COVID-19 as people have connected to

---

[17] https://www.pastortheologians.com/articles/2020/3/25/the-thing-about-online-church.

online worship. But other situations deserve our attention as well. For example, what about the active church family that relocates to a new state but continues to participate in small groups with their home church? Or the college student who worships with the church of her childhood online, since finding a new church is daunting? There are many examples of people whose only connection may be digital, and that connection can still be faithful. A college student or relocated family may choose to find a new church home, but why do they have to leave connections when we can bridge that gap for them?

Is online attendance less valuable to the congregation? Indeed, attendance is different but no less useful. And in fact, the digital expression of church allows people to continue their faith formation. A digital expedition calls us to make a mental shift, opening to the reality that just because we may not connect to online ministry doesn't make it less valuable for others and ultimately the Kingdom.

One more thing. A digital expedition enables connection that would not happen for those who are homebound and differently-abled. This is important, especially with the rise of loneliness and depression that can accompany a lack of mobility. Speaking of a virtual church experience, Douglas Estes writes:

> *The number of people who live on the margins of our world – and our class-stratified churches – is a lot larger than we think. However, in the virtual world, these people don't have to live on the margins, because at least at this point, there are no margins. No one can judge them based on race, class, age, or handicap because the virtual world masks everyone as handsome robots (or some other avatar representation), greatly lower the walls around the personal issues marginalized people face.* [18]

Being the Church and connecting as a congregation may look different as we consider the future, that is sure. But I think it offers opportunities to be with people at critical times in their lives. "An elderly man with senile dementia who follows a televised Mass in his care facility will participate in worship differently from the granddaughter who sits with him....and a young man recently paralyzed who cannot physically make his way to his parish church any longer yet finds

---

[18] Estes, Douglas (2009), *SimChurch: Being the Church in the Virtual World*, Zondervan, Kindle Edition, Page 235.

comfort in being present via Skype on an iPad that is taking his place in the pew...."[19]

But here is a critical thing to notice: even before screens and technology, people were present to one another to different degrees. There are degrees of being present, even if our English language struggles to express this. For example, if you and I attend the same church but sit in the front and you in the back, are we present together? Yes, we are, but it is very different than if you and I sat together in a house church with five others in a living room. Is one more valuable or more important? It is hard to say because being present together isn't a uniform experience.

My nearly ten-year experience of doing online discipleship groups has shown me that using a digital platform can even make us more present to one another. Gathering together and using technology like Google Hangouts or Zoom allows us to see one another and interact in a more present way than if we sat classroom-style, all facing forward and looking at one another's backs.

---

[19] Berger, Teresa (2017) @ *Worship: Liturgical Practices in Digital Worlds* (Liturgy, Worship and Society Series), Routledge, Kindle Edition, Page 22-23.

A digital expedition opens possibilities for deeper connections.

Mindset Shift: The Body of Christ as a Virtual Body

Being present to one another doesn't mean we have to sit in the same room. And in fact, the church was aware that being part of a church community wasn't limited to physical presence from the start.

The Internet, like the Body of Christ, has a mystical element to it. How the Web works are beyond (many) of our understandings, yet it does. The Body of Christ, the Church Universal, is beyond our understanding, yet it is an essential part of how Christians understand themselves.

Christians understand themselves to be Christ's Body on earth. We are his hands and feet doing works of justice and care. We are his eyes and ears, giving attention and comfort to one another during times of need. We are not an actual body but a virtual body, coming together worldwide regardless of our age, language, gender identity, or country. And after death, we speak of this Body as the Communion of Saints, another virtual image that invites us to see the mystery of God in the world.

In *The Virtual Body of Christ in a Suffering World,* Deanna Thompson writes of her cancer diagnosis and the support she received from people beyond her church and family, including a Jewish colleague who prayed to Jesus for her healing while on a trip to Israel. She writes:

> *What is also clear from this story is that our ever-expanding virtual networks are also going to push us to rethink the boundaries of the church, local and universal.*[20]

A digital expedition is in keeping with the Spirit of the Church, for "the Body of Christ has always been and will always be a virtual body." Throughout the world and throughout time, the Church is bigger than who sits in the pew on a given Sunday. From earliest times, clergy brought Communion elements of bread and wine to those home ill or unable to attend worship. While not present in the church, they were considered a part of the Body and were included in its sacramental care.

---

[20] Thompson, Deanna A. (2016). *The Virtual Body of Christ in a Suffering World, Abingdon Press.*

Mindset Shift: A Digital Expedition is about Relationships

Ultimately, a digital expedition isn't about technology. It is about relationships. Relationships, not technology, are at the center of digital ministry. As those on a digital expedition, we are called to make space not only in our churches but in our digital ministries for relationships that lead to an encounter with God in Christ and his Church.

We may begin this leg of the expedition with excitement, but we may also find a bit of overwhelm and trepidation. It is true, this part of the journey will call us to see the church beyond the building and enter into technology as much as we do theology. But because we value relationships and connecting people to the Author of Life, we can come to the journey hopefully.

So, don't ask if the church can exist online. It already does. Instead, ask what kind of church do we want to be online and where do we begin?

CHAPTER TWO

The Distinction Between Online Worship and Online Ministry

As we go on our Digital Expedition, we need to consider how what we do in person won't be identical to what we offer online. The difference between the two experiences requires us to think about how online ministry looks and feels different than in-person ministry. This chapter will discuss the essential concepts behind the differences, and in the next chapter, we will look at practical applications.

As we begin, we need to address a mental shift many of us have to make if our digital expedition is going to be successful: online worship isn't the same as an online ministry. *Online worship* is live-streamed or pre-recorded worship posted online. *Online ministry* is the much bigger container that includes worship but also so much more.

Many of us come to a digital expedition thinking that we offer online ministry when we post our worship service on Facebook or YouTube. And yes, it is an excellent first step. But honestly, it falls short of what digital ministry can and needs to be.

I recognize this shift can be tough to make. After all, we spend time and energy filming, editing, and posting a worship service, and it feels like we should be done. We have offered our best work – putting together music and message – and now it feels like any "next steps" are for others to take as they watch worship on Sunday morning. But what if there is something we have missed, and our work has just begun?

First, let's start by acknowledging why offering online worship is essential and a great first step.

Online worship matters in today's world. It is a place for congregations to connect with worship, prayer, and event announcements. I bring up announcements because even though I don't know what to do with the ever-growing list of Sunday announcements for in-person worship, I heard from people during

COVID-19 how announcements were a lifeline to connection in 2020.

If you offer online worship already, you should know, it is a good thing! Most churches launch on a digital expedition by posting worship online.

Did you struggle to take that first step? As I watched people post their worship services in the first couple weeks of the pandemic, I heard several clergy leaders reflect that they were not comfortable being on camera and were not interested in being "televangelists." This negative view of broadcasting (on TV or the Internet) is common, and churches who have used the Internet or TV are often looked down on, not only for their theology but also for the media used to get their message out.

Suppose you are a member of a smaller church and you had experience with online worship before COVID-19. In that case, it may be because – on a Sunday morning, as you were getting ready for in-person worship – you turned on the TV to keep you company. You ran into (depending on your age) Fulton J Sheen (called the first televangelist), Robert Schuller (and his California-based "Hour of Power" TV program), or Joel Osteen. For many in local churches, these examples kept them away from creating worship online, and it was only with the arrival of COVID-19 that they knew they had to step forward.

My experience was different. I began my digital journey when I served a church that videoed worship weekly and then burned CDs for purchase. The DVD ministry also posted the two worship gatherings on the church website (not YouTube) a week later. In 2008 that was a pretty exciting thing. We also moved into podcasting this season as podcasting was becoming a new, even more mobile way to reach a new audience. These digital ways to share scriptures, worship, and (yes) announcements enabled us to grow our outreach and connect more broadly than our small congregation.

At the time, I was aware of how unusual it was for a small church (under 200 in worship) to video weekly worship and offer it online later that week. The amount of technology used was not only costly but complicated. 2008's technology required multiple cameras and camera operators, a video booth, a director, and serious editing technology. It was a labor of love for a retired pastor and his crew to do this weekly, but it was out of reach of most smaller churches.

Five years later, in my work as Director of New Ministries for the United Methodist Church in Southern California, it was my habit to visit churches in person for worship each week. I enjoyed experiencing different congregations and their weekly worship. But one week, when I found myself home ill, I remembered my experience of serving a church that offered online (although delayed by a week) worship and searched for that morning's worship. Much to my surprise, few churches had added online worship, whether prerecorded or live streaming, even in Southern California.

All that changed with COVID-19. Small churches with no technology found themselves needing to go online THAT WEEK. And even those churches that had gone to the mat over installing a screen in the sanctuary realized they needed to connect with their congregation that was safer at home.

So, if your first steps toward digital ministry were to offer online worship, congratulate yourself. You took what is often the hardest step. I hope you see the benefits of providing online weekly worship.

During COVID-19, it was the only way many can gather. But you have probably already thought of why continuing online worship matters. Yes, it can connect your members when they travel or are on vacation. Yes, it helps your younger adults connect in a way that works whether they are away at college or were out too late last night to worship at 10 AM. But online worship also enables you to reach a whole new group of people.

Who are these people? Some we have already mentioned, including those who are differently-abled and unable to attend in person. But the use of technology allows new people to connect. For example, those from the deaf community can participate online with closed captioning. This is one way a church that does not have ASL interpreters can reach the deaf community. And, we are finding more and more that newer families can check out worship online to see if your community is a place for them to visit.

The church where I currently serve started

offering a live stream (worship is offered live as it occurs over YouTube) in 2019. Six months in, I was enjoying a cup of coffee at fellowship time after worship. A woman came over to me and said – "I know you! I see you on TV every week!" It took me a couple of minutes to understand she was referring to watching worship online for months before she and her husband came to join us for in-person worship. She has watched worship that morning online and was so moved by the music that she got dressed and joined us for our second worship in person. Online worship enables new people to connect in a comfortable way and on their schedules. Online worship can be a door to new people attending in person and new attendees who only worship online.

Online worship is a great place to start with your digital expedition, but it falls short of being a full expression of digital ministry. Why? For the same reason that offering in-person worship isn't the full expression of church and ministry. Worship is one aspect of church life, but it isn't the full or total expression. What is missing? Small groups, service to those in need, offering hospitality to newcomers, congregational care, and more cannot be left out of our digital ministry any more than they can be left out of our in-person ministry.

This is an important point: digital ministry is much more than posting online worship. It is a full expression of being the church but in a digital format.

So, what are the "basics" beyond online worship? What do we need in place to move from digital worship to digital ministry? Let's look at some important first steps.

First Big Idea – Keep it simple

One big issue in churches, in general, is how quickly things become complicated. As you imagine your online ministry, you must keep it simple. This may mean you don't offer everything online that you do in person. Think of your online ministry as incremental, growing in what it provides as you grow and build capacity.

When we move into a digital expedition, it is common to feel overwhelmed with all that we could do, but put that to the side and simplify your strategy. A simple strategy invites you to imagine what a newcomer to your digital expedition would need and start with simple offerings. Most of us would agree that a welcome, a connection to next steps, and a simple check-in – all of these are doable by anyone who has a heart for people – is an excellent place to begin. Don't make things complicated. Keep them simple.

Second Big Idea – Engagement

We will talk about this more in Chapter Five, but I wanted to get it on your radar now. Engagement is about connection and includes connecting people to God, to one another, and to church leadership. Engagement helps us see what is working in making connections and what is just something we thought was a good idea but has fallen flat.

You will have had experience with engagement with your in-person ministry, and you will find some overlap with your digital expedition. Pastor Nick Blevins[21] speaks about the importance of moving people along a pathway, starting with their awareness of your ministry to (many steps later) their investment

---

[21] https://nickblevins.mykajabi.com/.

in ministry. Each step on this pathway invites engagement with God, with others, and with the church. Each church benefits from understanding the steps along the way as people journey from awareness to investments. We will go into this more in chapter 5, but remember, engagement is as vital in a digital expedition as in an in-person one.

Third big idea – The Basics

The most significant fundamental component in digital ministry is your church website. Your website is your digital building and so how it looks to visitors is important. Take a moment to review it and make sure it is formatted for both desktop and mobile viewing, as 43 percent of those who look at your website will do so on their mobile device.[22] Your website should be geared toward visitors, and so it should be straightforward and easy to navigate. If you aren't sure how it looks to outsiders, invite a non-church member to look at your church's website and tell you what they see.

The most significant issues with websites

---

[22] https://gs.statcounter.com/platform-market-share/desktop-mobile-tablet/united-states-of-america.

are missing information (such as the location of the church; contact information for the pastor and senior staff; what to expect as a digital or in-person first-time guest; and information on family ministries, including any pre-registration information); outdated information (for example Easter information being featured during Advent): insider-focused (information is centered on communicating with the existing congregation rather than new people); and unhelpful information (statement such as "we met at Dave's home for small group this week, all are welcome" without us knowing who Dave is or where his home is located). Monthly updates allow you to keep your website up to date and serve a similar function to the weekly cleaning of your worship center.

If your website is your first step, social media is your second. Most churches pick one or two social platforms to communicate and promote events. When we talk about engagement, we will look at various options, but for now, take out your phone and look at your most used platform for social media. When was your last post? And how did it connect to others?

The most common use of social media by churches is as an announcement board. We tend to post "events" like upcoming worship or the Children's Ministry gathering. But social media – by its nature – is social, meaning connecting and relationship building. How do we move from using social media to announce events to building relationships?

First, respond to (most) every comment. If someone comments on a church post either publicly or privately, respond to them. If you ask a question (for example: What's your favorite Christmas Cookie?) and people respond, connect back to them (and who knows, you may end up with some cookies). Or, if you celebrate a local business or tell the story of a member doing good things, respond to those who connect. Responding is a simple thing, but it connects people.

Second, go live. This can feel intimidating! But my experience is it is a better experience if you have someone with you. After trying to up my connection to the congregation on social media, the church I serve began a twice-monthly "Coffee with the Pastors." It was a 30-minute conversation that gave that "behind the scenes" feel to the church's staff. Here were the pastors talking about how they celebrate the holidays, what kind of tea they enjoyed and what they were thinking about for the church. It took no prep (other than about 10 minutes to put together an outline) and connected us to over 300 people. Social media is a basic in a digital expedition, and it can be an opportunity to connect in meaningful ways.[23]

It is essential to know how your targeted demographic communicates digitally and uses that platform or app. In other words, go digitally to where the people you are trying to reach hang out in the digital world. For example, one demographic tends to use Facebook more while another demographic uses Snapchat more.

Fourth Big Idea – Next Steps.

An important part of a digital expedition is next steps. Earlier, we touched on why online worship isn't all we should be offering online. One big reason for that is that worship is the start (or maybe the middle), but it isn't the end. We want people not only to worship but to

---

[23] https://nickblevins.com/blog/2020/07/22/church-online-engagement-26-ideas-to-implement/.

grow, to serve, and to give. A digital expedition invites us to make someone's next steps easy, obvious, and strategic.[24]

Easy means offering a next step for connection that is doable – a comfortable step rather than a giant leap. If you have been attending online worship, your next step would NOT be an in-person small group at a member's home. There are just too many steps between an anonymous connection online and sitting in the living room of a stranger. A more appropriate next step might be to fill out a Connect Card and share your email information.

Obvious refers to something we mention weekly in online worship, an opportunity we post about on social media and our church website. For instance, inviting a newcomer to fill out a Connect Card and receive a gift – an announcement mentioned weekly with its own slide – is obvious.

Strategic refers to moving people from the first digital experience to a profession of faith and commitment. To be strategic means

---

[24] Stanley. Andy (2004), Multnomah, *7 Practices of Effective Ministry.*

we will know how we want people to progress and what stops them along the way. One of the challenges of a digital expedition is that while the barrier to entering into a digital ministry is low, the barrier to exit is also low. Knowing this means we need to have a easy, obvious, and strategic process, moving people toward Christ and his church.

With these big ideas in mind, now let's look at how this works in a local church.

CHAPTER THREE

Creating an Online Ministry That Connects

The world has constantly been changing. But it is human nature to lose sight of this and to think our own time is unique and more challenging. Every generation has debated how to deal with change and its new opportunities. Historically, communities (religious and otherwise) have considered how we deliver information, connect with others, and build community. Our generation may be unique in the amount of change we face, but knowing this is a constant in our society helps us make more informed choices.

One example: Plato held the view that written language was inferior to oral language. Along with other philosophers, he had *phonocentric* views – meaning that spoken language was richer and more fundamental – and this led him to hold disdain for written communication. Today we'd find this ridiculous, but I wonder about the many benefits we will see in the technology that today causes us to struggle? The world is changing and calls us to participate in the change.

The church has constantly been changing too. In *On Liturgical Theology,*[25] liturgical scholar Aidan Kavanagh reflected on how much worship has changed over time, noting that before the printing press, worship was heard and not read, experienced outside the doors of churches in courtyards and workplaces, and taking most of the day. What was normal for them would look like chaos to us. The church is changing and calls us to participate in the change.

In addition, today's in-person worship makes use of technology in such a seamless way that few of us notice. Additions such as lighting, heat and air-conditioning, microphones, and screens are part of most in-person worship experiences today, even

---

[25] Kavanagh, Aidan (1984), Liturgical Press, Preprint edition, *On Liturgical Theology* (Hale Memorial Lectures of Seabury-Western Theological Seminary, 1981).

though some may still find them debatable.[26] In addition, today's worshipers make use of contact lenses, cochlear implants, and artificial knees so that they might worship more fully. Technology, whether used to keep the temperature in our buildings comfortable or to allow our ears to hear the music played by the cello on Christmas Eve, is part of our everyday lives as we rely on its convenience.

During COVID-19, the church I pastored did outside worship. Our church is located in Southern California, and even in October, the weather was in the '70s. But one Sunday, it was overcast, and we had sprinkles. Just the fact that we might be in the '60s and have a moment of drizzle kept twenty people at home that day. We were so used to being comfortable and controlling our environment that the idea of being at its effect made us stay away. And while I did find it frustrating, I had to admit I have done the same thing at sporting events, preferring to stay at home to watch on television instead of sitting in the summer heat.

I share these examples to help us see that as we look at online ministry, it is just another

---

26 https://secondnaturejournal.com/of-mics-and-men-2/.

step toward reaching people and naming it "artificial" or "unnatural" ignores our use of technology to engage in in-person worship. Each generation sees new technology and reaps new possibilities. Our role as those on a digital expedition is to look at what is available and see how it can be used to further God's mission in the world.

Some call our period *the fourth revolution.* Stevan Harnad in *The Post-Gutenberg Galaxy*[27] says the previous revolutions were Language, Writing, and the Printing Press. Each of these technologies changed worship and furthered God's kingdom on earth. The positive opportunity in each technology opened doors to connect people with God and one another, and those communities that shunned the progress missed out.

As we turn to practical aspects of online ministry, I find Lee Rainie's and Barry Wellman's understanding helpful. They see the times in which we live as the 'triple revolution" – this included the Internet revolution, the social media revolution, and the mobile revolution.

---

[27] Harnad, Stevan (1991) Post-Gutenberg Galaxy: *The Fourth Revolution in the Means of Production of Knowledge.* Public-Access Computer Systems Review.

They write:

> *The combination of the Internet, mobile devices, and digital social networks has formed a new emerging infrastructure for relationships and community that previously only localized groups and organizations, like churches, could provide.*[28]

This triple revolution invites the church into broadcasting worship and relationships with people as we invite them to take their next steps with Jesus and his mission to the world. Our goal isn't to have the best or shiniest, but to have an online ministry that is easy to use, relational and doable. But how?

Online Engagement Pathway

Each ministry needs a pathway to take people from interested to committed. This is true whether you are doing in-person or online ministry.

If you've been active in an expedition team,[29] you've received tools (in the Essentials

---

[28] Anderson, Keith (2015), Morehouse Publishing; Kindle edition, *The Digital Cathedral: Networked Ministry in a Wireless World*, Page 872-873.

[29] greatestexpedition.com.

Pack of your expedition) to help you plan how you would partner with new people on their journey of faith (i.e., discipleship pathway, intentional faith development), moving them from their initial interest to becoming active and committed. Here is the good news: with some fine-tuning, it is probable that you can use this same pathway for online ministry. The overarching journey of moving someone from interested to committed looks different online but not so different than what you have in place won't be a helpful resource.

But if you do not have an engagement pathway, don't worry. An easy place to start is with Nick Blevins.[30] I find this engagement pathway easy to use and helpful in navigating a digital ministry. This pathway will be used throughout this chapter to help you develop a plan for online ministry.

The pathway has five steps. They are Awareness, Attention, Connection, Involvement, and Investment. Each step moves a newcomer into deeper connection with an online ministry. Let's look at these together.

---

[30] NickBlevins.com.

First Step in the Engagement Pathway: Awareness.

Awareness is the first step in moving into a relationship with your church's ministry. For in-person ministry, this is when someone hears about your church or drives past your building. For online ministry, it is when someone involved in your ministry shares a social media post or someone sees your Facebook ad. This also includes when someone searches for a church for help with an issue and is directed to your ministry website. We will look at this more in the next chapter when we look at evangelism.

Second Step in the Engagement Pathway: Attention.

While Awareness is a nodding acknowledgment that your ministry exists, Attention is when a person engages through looking at your website, connecting to your social media, or watching a worship service online. What ministry (next step) can be offered at this stage?

Engaging in this stage requires us to move through our default posture of a "broadcast" mentality. What is a broadcast mentality? If you grew up watching the news at 6 PM or your favorite show on Friday nights at 8, you are familiar with an experience that was a broadcast. A broadcast doesn't invite interaction. It is a presentation-only format. It is common for us, when we begin our digital expedition, to think of our online worship as a broadcast. But when we do, we miss the opportunity for engagement.

What might we do instead as we move from a broadcast mentality to an engagement pathway with those who connect online?

Attention: #1 Invite people to register and respond when they do.

Connect Card: If you offer online worship, highlight an online Connect Card for everyone (not just first-time guests) to fill out. A card can be created in google docs and posted to your website. This card is used not only to register attendance but to let you know prayer requests, register/sign-up for small groups, serving, etc., and any other needs.[31]

[31] Sample: https://umcv.org/connect-card.

We use a QR code to connect people to the card housed on our website, but you can also use a simple website address. If new people respond with their attendance or prayer requests, connect in the way they have provided (email, text).

This past week two new people watched our online worship. One provided a phone number and email, and so we tried the phone, only to find the mailbox full. Email was our next approach, and we sent a friendly welcome. The second person was the son of a church member who had left the church a dozen years ago due to a theological disagreement. We are now connecting him with a small group as he explores his faith.

Text "New" for Guests: Offer a gift for those new to your church and invite them to connect with a text. *Text in Church* offers a cost-effective service where a newcomer can text the word "new" to your Text in Church number. Our gift for new guests is an e-book from Amazon related to the current sermon series or a special topic. Other churches are making donations to a local charity in the name of the first-time guests as their gift.

Giving: Sometimes, people will not register attendance but will give. This should also be tracked and a response or a "thank you" acknowledged.

Recently a family donated with our online giving. This was our first contact with them – they had not filled out the Connect Card or Texted New. I sent a thank-you note to their home that week. The following week, I sent an email welcoming them to the church and inviting them to connect to this week's worship. They responded and filled me in on their story. We then set up a Zoom to meet with them and get to know them and their story. In addition, their two young children will get an Advent kit from our children's ministry next week.

I keep a running list of names, emails, addresses, and phone numbers of those who have connected in worship, and our pastors follow up with texts, notes, and emails inviting them to upcoming events and asking for prayer requests. In some churches, a staff person could fill this role, but in other churches, a layperson might fill this role.

Attention: #2 Respond on social media to likes and comments.

Your church should have a Facebook and Instagram account along with any other social media that makes sense in your context. When people like your posts or comment, connect with them. I also review new likes each week and message them if the connection looks like a real person (and not just a bot).

If someone asks a question on social media, we respond in twenty-four hours. If they email us, we respond in twelve hours. Some churches can do this faster. The key is to make sure you do it.

Attention: #3 Website.

We already spent time in Chapter Two on the importance of an up-to-date website. Websites are often where people first give ministry their attention, making sure the website is up to date.

The goal is to get this group to take their next step. So, ask: What opportunities (next steps) do we need to provide?

Third Step in the Engagement Pathway: Connection

The most significant difference between attention and connection is they have responded to our contact and are ready for more involvement. One of the most challenging aspects of both in-person and online ministry is how to move people from Attention to Connection. It is essential to know that this may take time, trial and error, and patience.

A person who has attended online worship and follows us on social media may never make it to the next level of engagement if we don't have a process, so what works?

Connection: #1 Decide where you want them to go FIRST.

There is no perfect "first step," and that is fine. Your church may feel you want them to connect to a small group first, while another church may decide they'd like them to come to the Discovery class where you go over church basics. But pick where you'd like folks to begin. Why? Because choosing your first step allows messaging to be clearer and more consistent. If there are three choices for next steps, that is usually two too many.

I find a Discovery Class is a great first step. It is a lot less time-intensive, and since everyone who attends is new, the playing field is level. An in-person Discovery Class is often a tour of the facility, an overview of ministries, a "what's unique about this church" discussion, and a Q and A with the pastor and/or lay leadership. Online our pastors host a time that features a slide show of our various ministries (small groups, prayer groups, service groups), a welcome from our youth leader and children's pastor, our values statement (ours is called *7 Things We Know To Be True*)[32] and a drone flyover of our campus to give them a sense of the in-person experience. The follow-up is an invitation to a small group, especially for newcomers and our women's and men's ministries.

Connection #2 Offer Seasonal Next Steps.

While I am a great believer in offering one next step to move people into involvement, I also know it doesn't work with everyone. This is why offering seasonal next steps can be helpful. What is a seasonal next step? At

---

32 https://umcv.org/about-1.

Advent, it might be a service project like participating in a Caring and Sharing tree or Advent study. At Lent, it might be a 40-days Reading Plan with a Facebook group; it might look like an online novel book study and online potluck in the summer. The big idea is to look at how to connect people in a way that makes sense in the context of the time of year. Offering one seasonal next step is a great way to try this out for your online community.

Connection #3 Listen and Learn

Keep track of people based on their place in the engagement pathway. Track how long it takes to move from connection to involvement. Make a note of what is moving people into involvement, and if something isn't working stop doing it. Ask those who are part of your online ministry what has been helpful to them. Listen, learn, and note who remains online and who moves to in-person connections. Be ready for some to remain only online while some may attend in person. Keep a focus on relationships and connections. Listening and learning from your online community will enable you to spend your time and energy making connections that matter.

Fourth Step in the Engagement Pathway: Involvement

In Chapter Three, we covered principles to keep in mind when designing steps for ministry – make each step **easy, obvious** and **strategic.**[33] This becomes especially important as we move into the Engagement Pathway. Moving from Connecting to Involvement is about attachment – people are becoming attached to the mission and people of your community. It can look like someone joining a small group, giving financially, or becoming involved in ministry. To help people take this next step, systems and communication need to be easy, obvious, and strategic. Here are some examples of how this can look:

Involvement #1 Keep Focused

If you have set up a Discovery Class (or whatever you have decided for your first step online), continue to invite people to this opportunity. I say this because it is easy to miss how powerful offering your first step consistently can be. Don't let your first step fall off the calendar or out of your usual communications

---

[33] Stanley. Andy (2004), Multnomah, *7 Practices of Effective Ministry.*

pattern. Instead, plan now to offer your first step monthly or at least every other month, and set that up for at least 12 months.

With online and in-person Engagement Pathways, you will find fewer people will participate than you'd like. That is for a variety of reasons. Some people will get stuck in earlier steps, some will fall off the pathway, and some will just take some time. Don't let this discourage you. Keep focused and learn what works.

The Rule of Seven says people need to hear something seven times before they respond. This is because the world is a noisy place where it takes a while for people to realize that they have a need (for a faith community) and that your community is a good fit for them. Offering your onboarding next step is key to being heard above the noise.

Involvement #2 Make it Easy

How easy is it for newcomers to connect? Is your website set up so they can find information on how to fill out a pledge card, join a small group or serve? Look at your website, your weekly email, your social media, and other tools from the perspective of a newcomer who is ready to take the next step. Make it easy and obvious.

In the church I serve, we have a basic form on our website to express interest in small groups. Those who fill out the form receive a follow-up call or email with additional information so they can join that week. For giving, we offer online giving and an online pledge card. Both of these normalize participating in the church's small groups and finances. Our social media is monitored, and those asking questions receive a quick response. Using services like Sign-Up Genius lets people register for events and enables us to respond to needs quickly without staff oversight.

Make it easy for people to take the next step.

Fifth Step in the Engagement Pathway: Investment

The fifth step in the Engagement Pathway is for those involved in your online community that step into serving as leaders and tithers. The smallest number of online participants will take this step, much like the smallest number of in-person participants. But how can you help this (next step) happen online?

Investment #1 Start with the End in Mind.

As you begin your digital expedition, start with the expectation that those who will be a part will want to become leaders in your church's ministry. With that expectation, you will begin your digital expedition with hope for what the Holy Spirit will do in people's lives.

Your role is to partner with the Holy Spirit and watch for participants who show leadership and commitment to God's ministry through your church's mission. Your attention will enable further development of people's gifts and leadership abilities.

Investment #2 Offer Leadership Opportunities.

In many in-person ministries, the clergy or paid staff take the lead. But for leadership growth, staff need to partner with others who show potential.

So, identify those who are growing into leadership. Invite them to co-lead an online class, invite an engaged newcomer to help with follow up or invite a new giver to record a stewardship moment. This connection will enable church leaders to mentor and help newcomers grow into leading ministry.

Your church may have the capacity to offer a leadership retreat, but if not, an intentional focus on mentoring newcomers is essential for online attenders to move into Investment. Believe that God can do this and be open to responding to those who follow his calling.

Attention, Connection, Involvement, and *Investment* are different on a digital expedition, but there is a familiarity to them if we have experience with this in person. In each step of the Engagement Pathway, we are inviting next steps of faith and relationship. This is something we can do with focus, planning, communication, and patience.

But before we welcome new people into our digital expedition, we need to look at how people find us and how we share the Good News.

CHAPTER FOUR
Digital Evangelism

The engagement pathway we are using starts with Awareness. This refers to people being aware that our church, our ministry, our fellowship exists. On the most basic level, awareness means people are familiar with our location. For instance, the church I serve is "across the street from the hospital" – this information helps those I meet in the community locate it. We are also the church that "runs that Facebook Ad that says: All Means All." These are two ways those in the community are aware of us.

But awareness can be much more. This chapter will talk about evangelism as awareness and look at strategies for connecting our digital expedition with others. In addition, this chapter will focus on starting a digital campus and creating teams for social media.

Recently, a Christianity Today article, "Coronavirus Searches Lead Millions to Hear About Jesus,"[34] shared that people were looking for faith in the early months of the pandemic. Internet searches on finding hope increased 170 percent, while clicks on ads about fear and worry increased 57 percent and 39 percent, respectively. Searches on prayer reached their highest level in five years.[35]

The Internet has made it easier to share faith, and a recent Barna Report noted that "58 percent of non-Christians said someone had shared their faith with them on Facebook, with another 14 percent reporting they heard a testimony through other social media channels.[36]

Of course, mass evangelism online reports not only its successes but its challenges. It takes a lot for people to move from a curiosity about Jesus to a daily walk with him and engage in His Church. For example, "While

---

[34] https://www.christianitytoday.com/news/2020/april/coronavirus-searches-online-converts-pray-cru-bgea-wmo.html.

[35] https://www.christianitytoday.com/news/2020/april/coronavirus-searches-online-converts-pray-cru-bgea-wmo.html.

[36] https://www.christianitytoday.com/news/2020/april/coronavirus-searches-online-converts-pray-cru-bgea-wmo.html.

60,000 people per day last year indicated on GMO's websites[37] that they had made decisions for Christ (either first-time commitments or re-dedications), the ministry was only able to track 5,244 people all year who connected with a local church after beginning their journey with Christ."[38]

This is where a church on a digital expedition has an advantage. Your church isn't a large organization but a local expression of the Body of Christ. As a local expression, it has an opportunity to connect people in a purposeful and personalized way. But where to begin?

Social Media

In today's world, every church that wants to reach new people needs to be on social media. But which social media? Facebook is the largest, so it is currently the best place for most churches to have a presence. Instagram and Twitter are second and third, and so if you have interest and energy, add those two into your church's social media presence.

---

[37] https://globalmediaoutreach.com/.

[38] https://www.christianitytoday.com/news/2020/april/coronavirus-searches-online-converts-pray-cru-bgea-wmo.html.

Facebook has 2.7 billion monthly users and 1.82 billion daily users.[39] That includes seven in ten US adults (69 percent). If we desire to reach people, we need to go where people are, and people are on social media.

Male users (19.3 percent) and female users (13.2 percent) between the ages of 25-34 are the biggest demographic group on Facebook.[40] Other helpful demographics:

- Seniors 65+ are the smallest demographic group on Facebook (4.8 percent)
- 23.8 percent of Facebook users are 18-24 years.
- 85 percent of Facebook users watch videos with the sound off.
- 84 percent of churches actively use Facebook as one of their major communication platforms.[41]

I make use of Facebook and Instagram for our church social media. I have tried

---

[39] https://www.statista.com/statistics/346167/facebook-global-dau/#:~:-text=During%20the%20third%20quarter%20of,percent%20of%20monthly%20active%20users.&text=With%20over%202.7%20billion%20monthly,most%20popular%20social%20network%20worldwide.

[40] https://www.omnicoreagency.com/facebook-statistics/.

[41] https://lifewayresearch.com/2018/01/09/most-churches-offer-free-wi-fi-but-skip-twitter/.

Twitter and Tick Tock, but that wasn't where our community was connecting. Our Family Ministries started with Instagram but has expanded to Facebook. I find using Facebook and Instagram for both the church and me personally works. Of course, as social media continues to evolve, it is essential to stay current. And, if you are excited about Snapchat or TikTok, go for it. Few churches are there, and your exploration may make a real difference in connecting. But for most of us, here are some guidelines:

Posts

Post daily and include a wide range of posts. You can explore "best times" to post (currently on Facebook, it is Wednesday at 11 AM and 1-2 PM, while for non-profits, it's Wednesday and Fridays 8-9 AM).[42] Monitor your posts and see when the best times are for those in your community.

Be aware that we tend to use social media as a broadcast medium. That is, we broadcast upcoming events and announcements. Social

---

42 https://sproutsocial.com/insights/best-times-to-post-on-social-media/#fb-times.

media is at its core social, meaning it is about connecting people. As you design your posts, consider how you can be social and connect with people. Here are some ideas:

1. **Powerful Short Videos from Worship** Each week, we create several evangelism posts for our Facebook page. One is a short (under two-minute) clip from the sermon.[43] Our social media manager will watch the message and edit it and add captions. This video is posted on our page during the week, and thirty percent of the time, we do a sponsored post to share it more widely than our 1,000 followers. A sponsored post is one form of advertising on Facebook, and for $1 a day, you can share something inspirational with a 10-25-mile radius around your church. Messages on hope, dealing with stress, and kindness rate highly with people watching, and adding a response button so people can connect lets people check out the church and share.

   Recording worship allows you to look at your service from an evangelism perspective and post short parts of worship to connect to those outside your church. Post testimonies from your members, powerful worship songs, and stories from your community that relate to

[43] https://sproutsocial.com/insights/best-times-to-post-on-social-media/#fb-times.

everyday concerns. Look at your weekly worship service with an eye toward what would connect to those who are not part of your community?

2. **Bible Verses and Bible Study**
   Each week post a Bible verse. Those outside the church are looking for more than a group of people. They are looking for a spiritual journey. A regular focus on scripture in social media posts conveys the centrality of scripture and its place in our lives. But what scriptures to post?

   The easiest first step is to find a regular place that provides quality graphics and verses. Some churches will use a resource like Canva and create their own. Others will use sources like SundaySocial.tv. Connecting the verse to either last week's focus or what is coming up next is a way to focus your posts.

   In addition to posting a verse, post a question such as "how are you living this verse today," or "what questions do you have about this verse?" Then collect the questions and thoughts and post a follow-up post from the pastor answering questions, sharing more about the verse, and encouraging others as they seek to live it out. This practical aspect of Bible study matters, especially from an evangelistic standpoint, so share scripture to connect.

3. **Ministry Partners Posts**

   Most churches have ministry partners. These are local groups that provide services such as housing and feeding those in need. Post about these and include how those in the community can help. Doing so shows those outside your congregation that Christians are engaged in the community and care for those outside their local congregation.

   We have two local ministry partners and two international ones. Each time they have an event, we post it on our Facebook page and encourage the congregation to attend. The church's hashtag #hereforgood is part of these posts as we stress our commitment to the community and those in need. These simple posts allow us to remember our values and to share and invite others to be part.

   One area this may be especially effective is if your partners aren't traditional church partners. If you are connected to the local LGBTQI Community Center, Anti-racism Groups, or Immigrant Advocate groups, these can alert your community to your church's concerns. Whatever partners your church has, share your support for them on social media.

4. **Sponsored Posts**

Facebook sponsored posts and ads are one of the easiest and cheapest ways to get the word out about your church. While some churches may still advertise in the local paper, magazine, or yellow pages, a sponsored post is a great way to attract newcomers to your congregation in many communities.

What is a sponsored post? A sponsored post is something you would usually post on your page but sponsoring (this costs a minimum of a dollar a day) shares it more widely than those who follow your page. We sponsor the weekly sermon video when it is on a topic that feels timely for our community (hope, forgiveness, stress). We also sponsor posts when a music clip or testimony from Sunday connected, and we want to get it out to a broader audience. I tend to run a sponsored post for five days and spend $5-10 dollars, focusing 25 miles around the church.

The best way to see if this works for you is to try it – take something you are excited about and sponsor it for $2 a day over 5 days. See if it gets comments, shares, or increases online worship attendance.

I noticed our online attendance grew in September and racked my brain to figure out why – it wasn't until I remembered we were trying some sponsored posts that I saw the connection. This has happened several times and has enabled us to grow our reach.

A Facebook ad is an ad you create and then pay to run. We have one we ran every other month in 2020 that enabled us to share who we are as a congregation with the broader community. Our ad says: "All means all. Everyone has stuff, and that's OK. Families come in all shapes and sizes. And, no one belongs here more than you. Online and In-Person worship, small groups, and more. We saved you a seat 'cause there is hope for everyone. #hereforgood." The photo in the ad was of a young woman with her back to us looking over the mountains.

When we first ran the ad, we looked at who it was reaching weekly. Facebook enables you to see who is seeing your ad by their age, gender, and other factors. That helped us tweak our ad for great effectiveness. We spent $1 a day for ads, but as we go into a season (Christmas or Easter), we will spend a bit more when people are looking to connect.

A word about using hashtags. Hashtags connect you with those outside of your community and engage your church in a wider conversation. They are a simple tool of engagement and can be used by any church on social media. Hashtags are also used as a way to brand your ministry for a season or a year or two.

We use the hashtag #hereforgood in all of our church posts, but we also use the city and state of our church (#valanciaca). Use hashtags for your upcoming worship series and any community events. It will help you in getting the word out. But beware: before you use a hashtag, do your research and see how the hashtag is being used already, you don't want to use a hashtag that connects to posts outside your focus or values.

Sponsored posts and ads are not where you want to begin your Digital evangelism, but don't be afraid to budget $30-50 a month to see the impact on your evangelism outreach.

5. **Other Evangelistic Post Ideas:**

- Community Gatherings such as parades and charity events
- Small groups that address people's needs, such as a newcomer's group, grief group, divorce support, or Financial Peace
- Events that are entry-level and exciting to attend, such as a Blessing of the Pets event, Christmas Children's concert, or Rise Against Hunger events[44]

Remember always to plan and provide next steps in posting and participating in these events. They are not one and done ideas. Think of these as stepping stones in a larger pathway of steps. As you explore sharing posts to connect evangelistically, keep in mind that

---

[44] https://www.riseagainsthunger.org/?gclid=Cj0KCQiAzZL-BRDnARI-sAPCJs72LwyKRUvsx8np1VN4sjxlmC0Eer1p8HnpYkqeNQ_gs-K4EYOUcr1t4aAk5_EALw_wcB.

the goal is connection. Building relationships takes time and cannot be rushed. People are not projects or items to fix, so focus less on numbers and more on the slow process of building relationships that lead to connecting. Learn as you go, and you will find connections with people who come to know Christ.

Digital Campus on Facebook

One of the biggest ideas for a brick-and-mortar church is to set up an online campus. Most churches wouldn't even consider this idea unless they were over 1,000 in worship, but you may want to reconsider with the use of the Facebook platform.

A digital campus of your church makes use of a Facebook Group. A Facebook Page is what most churches use, it is our front porch in social media, and anyone can connect and be part. A Facebook Group is private. It is a place where more engagement is possible because the circle is smaller.

In Nora Jones' book, *From Social Media to Social Ministry,*[45] Ms. Jones, who works for

[45] Nona, Jones (2020), Zondervan, *From Social Media to Social Ministry: A Guide to Digital.*

Facebook and is also a pastor, shares the idea of having a digital campus on Facebook. The book is worth a read if this idea intrigues you, but the big idea is that your Group is open to those who may never connect with your in-person campus but are interested in being part of your church.

What does a digital campus on Facebook look like? As the church I serve considers this idea, we are looking at a Lean Start-up model. So, instead of rolling out a big kick-off and hiring a pastor for the digital campus, our idea is first to grow the page with current members and friends (Phase 1); then roll out three weekly experiences online using Facebook Live, which would include a prayer time, a Q and A on last week's message and a short Bible study (Phase 2); and finally (Phase 3) invite those who are part to invite others. We are currently developing this (we are in Phase 1) and will launch Phase 3 around Easter, 2022.

What attracts me to this idea is that I am intrigued by what could happen with a lightweight-and-low-maintenance digital campus. Starting a digital campus costs nothing and can be a creative way to connect. This contrasts with what church planting is often about – securing space (which is often costly) and staff and learning how to connect in a new community. Church planting online builds on planting in a place filled with people with a far less expensive and risky strategy.

Social Media Team:

Depending on the size of your church, you may be the one doing your social ministry. Regardless of where you find yourself today, I invite you to build two teams.

Team #1

For your first team, which will focus on posting, I invite you to have the key staff, a social media manager, and leadership who will give feedback. Our social media manager posts for several churches and works 15 hours a week creating content and coordinating all of the postings. Previously the church secretary did this, but when we realized it wasn't her gift or passion, we made a new choice when COVID-19 hit. I recommend a social media manager for most churches unless your current staff has a passion (and time) for social media. Most social media managers can be hired for a reasonable amount and work remotely. The manager is responsible for ongoing posts, but the team can post when things come up that were not part of the week's schedule.

We work off a social media schedule that takes ten minutes to put together each week – this is where you are specific with the social media manager about what you'd like to see in the daily posts. The manager should give you guidance on what that could look like so it doesn't have to be entirely up to you. I do this weekly and use Google Drive to share my slides from worship, slides created for the sermon, and other ideas for the social media manager to put things together.

Team #2

The second team I want to encourage you to have is a group of church members and friends who like and share your posts. This team is a virtual team (bonus: no meetings), but they connect to those involved in social media, sharing what they find easy and helpful. Find these people by watching who likes and shares organically. Acknowledge them, inviting them to do it weekly, and following up with them to encourage their continued posts.

Recently, a church attendee shared a post from weekly worship with her testimony to how she experiences leadership at her church amid racial unrest in the community. Her words sparked a conversation with her friends who were interested in knowing more. This simple post allowed her to share her faith and to connect others to our community.

Finding a group of people who would function in this way took time. When I first invited people to share the church's posts, no one responded. But as I watched what was happening organically, I was able to see who had an affinity for this and encourage them, letting them know it wasn't an assignment but a way of helping others be aware of our community.

One last thing

There is a lot we didn't cover about online evangelism, but there is one thing we must still say: You must equip people to share what the church is all about with digital media.

The state of the world post-COVID-19 will continue to be a place where knowing Jesus matters. Online opportunities invite people to explore the faith in a comfortable way, which can benefit those searching. But congregations need to give simple tools to help people connect.

Here are a couple of tried and true ideas:

- As mentioned already, encourage people to share the church's posts. Give the direction at the bottom of the post: please like and share.
- Equip those with a commitment to the church to share resources with those in need. For example, if the church has a series on hope or relationship, encourage people to share it. We recently did a series on Living Easter Every Day and found 50 percent of those who signed up for the series shared the emails with friends and family not connected to the church.

In many ways, evangelism in the digital age is more natural. We just have to be intentional in reminding and inviting congregants to post, like, share, and comment until it becomes routine. We hear good news online and want to share it with others. On the digital expedition, evangelism may regain its rightful place in our faith.

CHAPTER FIVE

Engagement as Our Vitality Measurement

Churches count different things to judge how ministry is moving forward. A common one is: *how many were in worship this Sunday?* Baptisms and membership also can help us gauge how we are doing in reaching new people. Small group participation, number of returning first-time guests, and giving are often part of the equation to provide us with a sense of the congregation's vitality. When we measure any of these things, behind them is a desire to measure engagement.

Engagement "defines the level of interest and involvement of a person, whether they are Pastors, Lay-leaders, Staff or your Congregation, as well as their level of enthusiasm and commitment to your church and its mission."[46] This is true whether it is in person or online, but in-person engagement is more natural for us to spot. We can see the energy in the smile of a newcomer who has finally found a church home; we can see the tears of worshipers as they cry out to God in the midst of a local tragedy. Online, we miss these cues and miss the natural connections we make between numbers, people, and engagement.

One of the churches I served had two worship gatherings on Sunday morning. My first month, I noticed something peculiar; after I said goodbye to the last person in the greeting line at the end of the second worship hour. I was often one of the last people still in the building. I had never experienced a church like this – usually, we had to ask people to leave as they stayed so long laughing and enjoying time together. This lack of connection among the congregation showed me that engagement was low. I could see it with my eyes.

How do we measure online worship engagement? How do we get people to connect

---

[46] Davis, Walter Franklin (2019), Independently published, *Rebooting Church: The Future of Church - "Digital-Church"* - Starts Here!, Page 188.

to people and God with more than online worship? How do we move people from consuming what a church staff produces each Sunday online for worship or during the week on social media and move them into connection?

I have been thinking about this for a long time. For years I taught an online discipleship workshop. For 6-weeks, I help laity and clergy look at one model of discipleship called a Discipleship Huddle. One week was spent talking about the importance and power of being a disciple in relationship with other disciples in a local church. This is my favorite week to teach because it moves discipleship into a fuller context.

Too often, it feels as if discipleship has become a personal journey, something someone does on their own at their home on their schedule. For example, many Christians have a morning practice of reading the Bible and prayer. There is nothing wrong with that (in fact, there is a lot that is right about it), but if my discipleship journey excludes connecting with other Christians as I study, pray and serve, my journey will be less rich than it might have been. People and a connection to them make a real difference in a faith journey.

The scriptures call us to be connected and never suggest that this connection, this engagement, is optional. In the scriptures, there is a list of ways we are to connect on our journey of discipleship, often referred to as the "one another's." These scriptures call us to look at what Biblical engagement – whether in-person or online – looks like. Here is a (partial) list:

- *Be at peace with each other* (Mk. 9:50)
- *Wash one another's feet* (John 13:14)
- *Love one another* (John 13:34, & 12 other references)
- *Be devoted to one another in brotherly/sisterly love* (Rom. 12:10)
- *Honor one another above yourselves* (Rom. 12:10)
- *Live in harmony with one another* (Rom. 12:10)
- *Stop passing judgment on one another* (Rom. 14:13)
- *Instruct one another* (Rom. 15:14)

- *Accept one another, as Christ accepted you* (Rom. 15:17)[47]

This list always inspires me to engage more fully as a disciple and see my faith journey not as a solo journey but as one that calls me to be engaged with a community. I share this list and its call to us because we will face some challenges as we talk about our digital expedition. But let's not dumb down engagement online because it takes some creativity to imagine what being community online means. Instead, let's look at what possibilities await us.

Engagement Big Idea One: Study Current Engagement and Adapt

If you have an online worship service, how many people are watching it? That is a

[47] The rest of the list: "Greet one another with a holy kiss" (Rom. 16:16, 1 Cor. 6:20 and 2 Cor. 13:12).
"When you come together to eat, wait for each other" (1 Cor. 11:33)
"Have equal concern for each other" (1 Cor. 12:25)
"Serve one another in love" (Gal. 5:13)
"If you keep on biting and devouring each other, you will be destroyed by each other" (Gal. 5:15)
"Let us not become conceited, provoking and envying each other" (Gal. 5:26)
"Carry each other's burdens" (Gal. 6:2)
"Be patient, bearing with one another in love" (Eph. 4:2) .

tricky question. If you post your worship on Facebook, you could think 1000 people are watching your 40-member church worship. Only as you dig deeper that you might learn most all of those are one-second views. Counting those is like counting the number of cars that drive by your church on Sunday morning as part of your worship attendance.

So how do you begin to understand your current engagement? Facebook and YouTube offer analytics on their sites. Spend 30 minutes reading through what they offer. Don't worry if it is a lot of information. As you read and study, you will begin to formulate your questions.

Facebook Example:

Here is a snapshot of worship on Facebook on two Sundays in November 2020, along with some options for greater engagement :[48]

Worship on November 22:

- 107 1-second views
- Four 1-minute views
- Seven who "engaged," meaning they liked or shared the post.

[48] Valencia UMC, Valencia, CA

Worship on November 29:

- 108 1-second views
- Nine 1-minute views
- Six who "engaged," meaning they liked or shared the post

By tracking analytics, this church has found that Facebook isn't where people go to see this church's worship service. Because of that, they have gone back and forth about the time it takes to upload to Facebook and have had weeks where, instead of uploading, they shared a link to worship hosted on YouTube. In this congregation, analytics showed that higher engagement was found in posts throughout the week where more bite-size parts of worship were shared.

For example 3 videos from 11/22 worship had:

- 39 1-minute views and
- 42 engagements

Knowing this enables the team to focus on shorter videos to connect and engage. In November, the highest engagement was with a Facebook Live called *Christmas Coffee with the Pastors* – a behind-the-scenes conversation with the church's two pastors. Seeing this, a monthly conversation was calendared.

YouTube Example

YouTube's analytics are very helpful. They enable you to see unique views (so you don't count someone numerous times if they stop and start watching) and allow you to see when people tune in to a premiere video and how long they watch.

Initially, we created a worship service online that ran the same amount of time as our in-person worship. But it quickly became apparent that those who watched our modern worship service turned in late (to miss announcements) and left after the sermon. We adjusted what we did for greater engagement. Our traditional worship service stayed the same until we noticed six months into the pandemic that people were tuning out after the sermon, so we adjusted our time. Based on comments and analytics, our latest addition was to offer the sermon alone each week as its own YouTube video.

We were also initially frustrated with the lack of comments on our YouTube page. We knew people were watching, but we received little engagement in the chat even with a weekly host. As we learned that most people watched on their Smart TVs, which didn't show the chat function, we recognized engagement needed to look different.

As you begin, study your current engagement. And don't worry if you don't know what it all means; as you start tracking you will see patterns and gain understanding. It takes patience and a good 6-9 months to see trends. This is also where contracting with a communications professional can be helpful.

Engagement Big Idea Two: Help People Connect Beyond A Like

Analytics are helpful, but we will find them unsatisfying, confusing, and even discouraging for most of us who got into ministry to connect to people. An upload of a worship service to Facebook takes real staff time, and finding out only a small number watched more than a minute feels terrible.

So, don't track engagement with Facebook or YouTube tools. A like on a post doesn't do much for authentic engagement. Use their analytics to compare each week to the previous week to stay on top of any changes (for example, if no one watched your YouTube worship, it may have been a corrupted file), but look for a more people-centered way to track.

Here are some ideas:

1. In Online Worship Invite a Response

Sometimes we don't have engagement because we don't invite it. Make sure you are inviting people to connect each week.

And then focus on making that connection an easy step to take. Make use of slides in online worship with a website address so people can register attendance. Use a phone number to text so you can welcome newcomers. And create a QR code (for free, online) to make it easy for people to sign up for an event.

Any online worship services will need opportunities for people to respond, and hosts online can take the lead by highlighting these opportunities in the chat. These can include:

- **A Connect Card:** A neighboring church was trying to figure out attendance at its online service and asked how we were doing it. When I explained our Connect Card, they realized their oversight. Invite people to register their engagement by sharing who they are, who is participating with them, and what prayer requests and needs they have. This simple step, which we repeat weekly, has enabled us to connect with phone calls, food, and prayer. It has increased our engagement with those who watch.

- **Giving Online** – Giving online has grown over the past ten years. Today it is essential for people to give without writing a check or being in worship when the plate is passed.

- **Connect to the Preacher for a Resource** – I like to offer a resource as part of my sermon. It might be a PDF worksheet to take the topic deeper or an e-book. I'll say something about the resource in my sermon and have a specific email for them to contact. You can also do this with a text. Let them know if they aren't watching it when the message is released, they can still receive it and how.

2. In Social Media, pose a question

Depending on the size of the church, getting people to respond on social media can be difficult. The first way to address this is by asking questions, sharing stories, and celebrating people.

- **Have a question of the week** – For example, if the sermon was on HOPE, ask, "where did you find hope?" Questions don't have to be serious. Asking your favorite ice cream on the 4th of July weekend or your favorite way to carve a pumpkin in October gets people interested. Our most successful questions have connected to commemorative days like Teacher's Day, when we have invited people to share what teacher made a difference for them.

- **Sharing Stories** – Who has a testimony or faith story to share? These can be simple and short (under two minutes). Maybe your story is from a child who is having her last cancer treatment or a mom who just enrolled her kids in your programs or found you online. Stories make it personal. In the church in which I serve, we have a hashtag we use, #hereforgood. One year we did a monthly post of someone who was #hereforgood by their service in the church and the community. These stories were fun to share and helped us get to know one another.

- **Celebrating People** – Each year, we give an award called, The Towel and Basin Award. It goes to the individual, couple, or family who has served God in an exemplary way in that year. This year, we videoed their receiving the award and shared it on several social media platforms. Whom can you celebrate as a way to inspire others that God uses everyday people?

These practices will help you build engagement, but consider adding a Facebook Group if you find it slow going. Groups are private communities, and because they are smaller, they can help create comfort with entering and engaging. This has been our experience as we have found under a dozen people responding on our Page and thirty people responding in our Group.

3. Offer Online Experiences Connect and Teach

Create opportunities for those who are new and for people who are part of your online and in-person communities to connect. These can be ongoing small groups, seasonal small groups, one-time workshops, or membership classes.

- **Small groups/seasonal small groups:** A church that values ongoing discipleship in a community context can use online groups for weekly meetings. The value of online groups – especially in communities where people have long commutes and childcare issues – can connect people in ways that in-person groups may not. As Margaret Wertheim suggests, we might just "do better with the (Internet) than we have done with the physical world."[49] The goal is that people living across the country from one another, and those whose health keeps them homebound, can find community together.

- **One-time or Theme Workshops:** A digital ministry allows us to offer online workshops to connect with new people, engage those within our ministry circle and learn together. We recently did two workshops on racism that included people not usually at our in-person events. We hosted a four-week Mindfulness Meditation gathering that drew people from five different states. Relationships were built, friendships were rekindled, and those without a church connection found a warm welcome into a diverse community. Some of this will translate to in-person relationships, but others will remain as online connections. Consider topics around mental health, which are always important and may receive little attention in the church. Knowing the hot issues in your local community and the

[49] From Margaret Wertheim, *The Pearly Gates of Cyberspace: A History of Space from Dante to the Internet* (New York: W. W, Norton & Co, 2000), 285, quoted in Thompson, Deanna A. (2016), *The Virtual Body of Christ in a Suffering World,* Abingdon Press, Page 8.

nation will help you offer opportunities currently top of mind for people.

- **Membership Class:** Of all the things we offered in our digital ministry our Membership class surprised me most. Our membership class was led by six different leaders who brought various topics (spiritual gifts, finance, structure) to those joining the church. The course was three sessions over three weeks. When we re-imagined it online, we looked at doing one session and prerecording all the presenters. Prerecording everyone allowed us to put together segments hosted by the pastors who kept things moving forward for those online. Doing it this way enabled people to see each other and share more so that even during the pandemic, we received new members.

Engagement is about connection. It is the opposite of passive consuming and enables connection to live out the "one another's" together. Experimentation is vital but the goal is clear: connection.

A Postscript as We Talk about Engagement:

In the church, engagement is often about to help to get people to engage with the church and its ministry. This is important. But a digital expedition offers tools for its travelers, tools that help travelers connect – and engage – with God.

The use of apps for prayer, Bible Study, evangelism, and meditation are some of the most exciting ways to engage people with God. God is found not just in a church building but during our commute, our walk, or morning shower. Liturgical multi-tasking is engagement.

> *The question is whether the prayerful encounter with the Holy One can so easily be paralleled with other daily routines? Once again, this is not a problem of the digital age alone. Weaving baskets while reciting psalms, as desert fathers and mothers did, or praying the Divine Office out of a breviary while on a train ride, as priests in the early 20th century did, were also forms of liturgical multi- tasking.*[50]

The Pray-as-You-Go app[51] invites people to center and to become still. The Divine Office app[52] has an audio function to enter into prayer

[50] Berger, Teresa (2017) @ *Worship: Liturgical Practices in Digital Worlds* (Liturgy, Worship and Society Series), Routledge, Kindle Edition, Page 28.

[51] https://pray-as-you-go.org/.

[52] https://divineoffice.org/welcome/.

with a community as you pray morning prayer. The Read Scripture app[53] takes you through a reading plan with engaging videos, while the *Our Bible*[54] app lets you hear alternative voices share Bible study topics. These apps can be used on your own (self-guided) or as part of a practice with others. Interestingly, these apps are growing in popularity, possibly because "prayer and smartphone habits work well together."[55]

"At the heart of any real church – regardless of the world in which it exists – must be people called by God to be his servants, proclaimers, apostles, and bridge builders to the world. Whether those people represent themselves in middle-class golf shirts and summer dresses, in coarse camel hair, or with 3D high-resolution avatars may not matter. What matters is that they get involved and take hold of their calling to be ministers in their community. Can virtual churches encourage people to participate in ministry? Can they get them to participate as

---

[53] https://www.readscripture.org/.

[54] https://www.ourbibleapp.com/.

[55] Author unknown.

much as in real-world churches? How about more than in real-world churches?"[56]

As we journey on our digital expedition, this is an intriguing thought for the 21st century.

[56] Estes, Douglas (2009), *SimChurch: Being the Church in the Virtual World*, Zondervan, Kindle Edition, Page 233.

CHAPTER SIX

Hybrid Model

In the book *Weird Church,*[57] authors Beth Ann Estock and Paul Nixon share the nineteen models of church they are currently seeing. These include the Neighborhood church, the Dinner Party church, the Mission Base Camp church, and the Cathedral. Each of the nineteen models shares the same mission: to be church. But each is a unique expression that God is using to reach new people. It is both exciting and intimidating to see all the diversity, but it is how the Spirit moves.

Andrew Jones[58] and Carol Howard Merritt have also shared lists of emerging church

---

[57] https://www.amazon.com/Weird-Church-Welcome-Twenty-First-Century/.

[58] https://tallskinnykiwi.typepad.com/tallskinnykiwi/2009/12/10-types-of-emerging-church-that-no-longer-upset-your-grandfather.html?cid=6a00d8341c5bb353ef0120a79562d2970b.

models.[59] Merritt's list includes New-monastic Communities and Podcast Churches. Not all of the churches on her list still exist (including the Internet churches she mentions), but her focus, like that of the book Weird Church, is to open our minds to new, fresh and alive forms of church.

I led a House Church that met in my backyard garden for several years. We were connected to a local brick-and-mortar church and reached people who were tired of traditional worship or who were church leaders unable to worship while working on Sundays. In addition, our neighborhood friends joined in as well. It was a wonderful expression of the Holy Spirit.

But here is the thing. Most churches, even if they are a fresh expression of today's church, are ONE expression. They are a traditional expression of church, meeting Sundays at 10 AM, or Neo-Monastic, practicing a rule of life together each morning and serving the community. They are a church that meets in a backyard garden or a church full of young adults gathering at a coffee shop. While most churches have some

---

[59] https://www.christiancentury.org/blogs/archive/2011-11/ten-church-models-new-generation.

kind of Internet presence, the focus isn't about gathering online and in-person. Websites are used to list when and where the group meets, but Zoom isn't where they worship.

All of that has changed. Regardless of its type, today's church has found itself needing an online presence, not just as a billboard to broadcast its activities but as a way to gather, worship, disciple, and more. The future is hybrid. The future is both/and.

Of course, there is a lot of debate around this. Smaller churches that moved online may not have the resources to do both in-person and online. Pastors doing both in-person and online worship report burnout and exhaustion.[60]

In addition, a recent Pew Study shared:

"The coronavirus outbreak also does not seem primed to usher in a permanent rise in virtual worship. In fact, among U.S. adults who recently watched religious services online or on TV, a larger share say that they intend to watch virtual services less often (28 percent) rather than more often (19 percent) after the pandemic passes. About half (53 percent) say

---

[60] https://www.barna.com/research/covid-19-pastor-emotions/.

they will watch services online at about the same rate as they did before the pandemic."[61]

So why do we want a hybrid model on our digital expedition? Why not just go back to what we had?

I hope this book has helped you see how essential connecting online is. A digital expedition enables you to connect with those seeking Christ, whether they are differently-abled, dealing with health issues that keep them at home, or looking to check out your church before an in-person visit. A Digital expression of church is as valid as any expression, and in today's world, it is one way the Holy Spirit is moving.

The church I serve set up live stream worship a year before the pandemic – our average attendance on live stream was 50 people. Some of those were our college students looking to connect, some were those checking out the church before a visit; some were previous members who hadn't found a home in their new community, and all of them needed connection that a hybrid model offers.

---

[61] https://www.pewforum.org/2020/08/07/americans-oppose-religious-exemptions-from-coronavirus-related-restrictions/.

So how do we live into a hybrid model?

First: Know your limits and gather your team

If you are participating in *The Greatest Expedition,* you are part of an Expedition **TEAM**, meaning you are among people with various gifts. Take time to know each other and share who you know beyond your current team members who might be part of your digital expedition. This is an opportunity to invite the artist, the film editor, the sound nerd, and the person with an eye for set design. In some churches, these people don't have a place to serve. A hybrid ministry offers them this opportunity.

We use a small team for digital worship, discipleship, and social media. Currently, our team is a social media manager (15 hours per week), an editor who edits the music video for worship (5-10 hours per week), a graphic designer who creates slides for monthly worship themes, worship announcements, and social media (1-2 hours per week), and a worship editor who puts all the pieces together and uploads to YouTube and Facebook (6 hours per week). We also have a couple of film editors who can create unique videos such as onsite mission videos. Some of these roles overlap with our in-person ministry (especially graphic designers and social media managers).

In addition, our pastors work with small group leaders who use Zoom to gather their groups. Look at your younger people and older people for the skills, time, and excitement to be part of your team.

Our team has both staff and volunteers, and when we moved into a hybrid model, we needed to realign our budget and staff. We no longer have a full-time secretary for bulletins and phones but used those funds for our social media manager, who works remotely. Our staff who put together graphics for in-person worship added in video editing, and several others shifted work for a better flow. Don't be afraid to look at your budget and make changes for a hybrid ministry model.

Second: Gather the Basics

I am not a tech person and have had to rely on those around me. You should, too! But here are a couple of basics:

Recording and Editing Capacity:
If your church hasn't invested in cameras to

record or live stream, they will need to make that leap for a hybrid ministry. Talk to those on your team with interest and expertise in this area, or visit a church that has done this for help. Editing software comes on most newer computers. We use Apple's iMovie, which is easy and intuitive.

Live Stream and Broadcasting Capacity: Live streaming enables worship to be recorded while broadcast live in real-time. Live streams can be hosted on YouTube and Facebook, among other platforms. Some churches that began online worship during COVID did so by live streaming to Facebook or by using Zoom. As churches move into a more hybrid model, YouTube and Vimeo are being utilized. The benefit of using some type of live stream is it cuts out the need for video editing (except for any additional clips you may make use of during the live stream) and it enables those online to experience the energy of an audience. The downside is that streaming what is going on in a room can feel like an afterthought, and those who watch online may feel second class.

Some churches would rather pre-record what they are going to post. This enables a church to create something that is specifically for an online audience. It also allows a video editor to edit out mistakes and tighten up transitions, such as people walking to the microphone to speak. We do both and embed live stream and recorded worship on our website, which takes people directly to YouTube.

Hosts and Connecting:
As you consider how your model will look, check out opportunities to connect with people online. You can use the chat feature of YouTube or explore Church Online and Free Church Online. Use hosts in the same way you would greeters for your in-person experience. I recommend having two hosts for each service to build engagement.

Third: Make Decisions about In-Person and Online Worship

The most complicated part of a hybrid model is worship. Once you have the tools, you need to ask: Does our online worship look the same online as what it does in the room?

There are various thoughts on this, and we all need permission to experiment and learn what works best. With the right equipment, it is easiest to have a hybrid model that streams what is happening in the room during worship, but that may not be most effective. Being in the room is different than watching on a screen in your home; how different depends on who you are asking.

People feel passionate about this. Some believe that in-person worship and online worship are so different that you should never duplicate what is happening in-person for the online congregation. Others want those who watch at home to see exactly what those in the room experience. How do you figure out what works best in your context? Here are a couple of ideas.

Ask those who are watching online. When we were only online during the pandemic, we used a combination of new music that our musicians would record at their homes and videos we had from previous worship services. Some people commented they loved the feel of those recording at home and others remarked how great it was to see the whole choir or band and hear a favorite. Asking those who watch mainly online what works for them may not give you answers, but it will provide you with information upon which to decide.

Use YouTube Analytics. If you are doing a hybrid model now and are live streaming exactly what happens at in-person worship, review your analytics. When do people tune in? When do they leave the live stream? Shortening up what you offer will require you to prerecord worship but doing this enables you to focus only on those online instead of splitting attention between those in the room and those online.

Offer Two Separate Offerings If You Can. Currently, we record worship on Wednesday. We do announcements, prayer, sermon, and a stewardship moment each week. What we record is specifically for those who will watch online. Our in-person worship is outside and not recorded. It is for those who attend in person. Are they that different? Not really. Some weeks the music is different. Some weeks the sermon is a little long online. Of course, the transitions are better online, but the big difference for us is who we are addressing. Are we talking to those online or those in the room?

If you can do two worship offerings – one for those who attend in-person and one for those online – that is ideal. But is it practical? Probably not for most churches. If it is not practical for you, and you will be providing one service that is both in-person and online, try these:

- Go over camera angles and get tighter shots. Long shots of the sanctuary can feel impersonal and can make the online experience less engaging. Figure out where preachers and musicians need to stand to be seen online best.
- Don't forget the lighting. Light is often very different in person than what is required online. This may mean that additional lights are used, which may block the view of those in the room.
- Go over transitions. Online we never need to see anyone walking up to the microphone. Train those who operate the cameras to focus on presentation slides (if you have a theme slide for the series, this is easily done) and not backsides.
- Work on sound. Is the sound mixed for online listening? This may take extra equipment, but it needs to happen since post-production cannot adjust a too-quiet microphone.
- Train speakers on how to speak to those in the room and those online. Where are the people seated? What camera is the one you should address? This takes practice and

adjustments, so invite those who lead each week to review the video to learn what works and what doesn't.

- Have two hosts engage people online as you offer both in-person and online work to engage those attending. Why two? Two people can model what online engagement looks like as they connect and invite others into the conversation.
- Do a hybrid of your hybrid. Depending on what you find, you might want to consider recording worship, editing it, adding in a sermon that is addressed only to the camera, and posting it a week later. This enables whoever is the preacher for the week to narrow who is being addressed (either those in the room or those online), which may be more effective.

Worship and video tools will continue to evolve as the technology grows. But remember, you don't need the newest or the most complicated system, just a system that lets your digital expedition reach people hungry for Jesus who are already gathered or yet to be gathered. Don't make it more complicated than it needs to be, and know that you will grow in your confidence and skill as you do hybrid ministry.

Fourth: Connect for Discipleship (Classes and Small Groups)

Years ago, someone contacted me to help them set up a way for their seniors to pray together online in the evening. No one had computers, and so we used FreeConferenceCall.com. It worked perfectly, and today that same group uses it not only for prayer but for Bible study and small groups. I share this because you don't always have to go video-based. A hybrid model invites a variety of tools, including conferences calls and video connections like Zoom.

What other tools are available? Connect on the YouVersion Bible App, which allows your small group to read scripture together and comment. Other apps like Read Scripture, Lectio 365, and the Divine Office, also enable people to connect and grow their spiritual connections. Tools such as Marco Polo, Facebook Groups, and Facebook Messenger can also connect people together. Spend an hour with your team assessing the tools and what would work best for your church. Don't make it complicated, and don't feel you need the newest app or tool.

Hybrid discipleship groups can combine the best of both worlds by meeting online and in person. Using a Smart TV or a screen that can connect to WIFI and laptops enables a hybrid model that makes space for everyone to grow. Combining in-person and online allows a group to continue connections even when members have moved, don't have childcare, or have challenges with transportation.

Fifth: Connect for Prayer

Prayer, by its nature, invites people to participate when they are not together, so prayer may be the most natural of our hybrid models. Prayer chains have been in use by churches since landlines were the only ways we had to connect, which points to how natural this hybrid is.

Expand your prayer ministry by inviting people to list their prayer requests on your Facebook Group (not Page) on a Tuesday morning and then go live on Wednesday praying for those in need. Having a regular rhythm allows people to participate and connect. Use Zoom, email, text messaging, and phone calls to connect people for ongoing prayer.

Sixth: Bring People Along

Not everyone will understand why hybrid ministry is important. Many are grounded in an in-person expression and will doubt that using online and in-person ministry is necessary. Don't let this hold you back in your digital expedition.

In some ways, this challenge reminds me of the one faced when congregations installed screens in their sanctuaries. While many churches saw how helpful screens could be, many did not and worried that adding a screen would take us further away from being an authentic expression of church.

But as more churches installed screens, I saw something interesting happen: those who kicked off the use of the screen the first Sunday in November (All Saint's Day) fared better. Why? Because using the screen to show photos of beloved family and church members showed the technology in the best light and helped people see how technology could meet our relational needs.

As you begin your digital expedition, know that you will be most effective in bringing people along when you collect and share stories of the positive impact your hybrid ministry is having. When you are doing new things (such as going on a digital expedition), sharing stories help create a new culture in which a difference is made through technology. Let people know how a beloved church member could continue to worship with her congregation after her cancer made her unable to attend in person. Let people know how college students stayed connected through their small groups. Sharing stories will go a long way in helping people see why a hybrid model of ministry matters.

Hybrid ministry isn't the future. It is the present. We are called to be online because God uses digital ministry to reach people and grow their faith. As we put together our own hybrid ministry, we know it will invite us to experiment, to learn, and to reach out for others' expertise. And in doing so we will be part of what God is doing in today's world.

POSTLUDE
Top Seven Ideas

As we journey on this digital expedition it is easy to get caught up in the how do's:

- How do we do worshipful online worship?
- How do we engage with online participants?
- How do we help our current congregation understand why digital ministry matters?

The "how" matters, and it can take our energy and focus.

But I like us to end with a focus on the what: The Church. The Church is Christ's Body on earth, and that Body is virtual. The virtual Body of Christ has always been us, the people of God. We are that Body together – whether we meet only online or have a hybrid model where people are the Church together online and in-person. The Church – whatever its type and however it meets – is "a people who have learned how to be faithful to one another by our willingness to be present, with all our vulnerabilities, to one another."[62] This is key, and a church rises and falls by its relationships and sincerity. Our presence online, like in person, needs to be marked by truth. "Our presence as digital ministers should be compassionate, engaging, inspiring, accessible, and informative. But above all it must be real. It must be an authentic representation of ourselves as real human beings who are people of faith."[63]

The church has always been changing form. And as the form changes, we have nothing to fear. When John Wesley began his ministry in America, his new way of doing church was not embraced by those who held fast to tradition. "Were these new Methodist charges real churches? What impact would they have in a brave new world?"[64]

---

[62] Hauerwas, Stanley (2001), *The Hauerwas Reader,* Duke University Press Books; Annotated edition. Page 553.

[63] Estes, Douglas (2009), SimChurch: *Being the Church in the Virtual World, Zondervan,* Kindle Edition. Page 229.

[64] Estes, Douglas (2009), *SimChurch: Being the Church in the Virtual World,* Zondervan, Kindle Edition. Page 231.

Wesley "... established churches as nodes of spiritual growth and discourse rather than just as buildings where people meet. This is why one man, Wesley, with several hundred circuit riders in the nineteenth century, today boasts a staggering seventy-five-million spiritual descendants in the United States alone – far more than anyone of his day could ever have imagined possible."[65] Wesley was not afraid, and we don't need to be, either.

I had an opportunity to talk to two people who are part of my congregation and work in Hollywood – Chris Ender[66] and Cathleen Taff.[67]

Chris reminded me how an online worship service breaks down barriers for new people to explore the faith. His words reminded me of my journey to connect with a church and how awkward I felt that first Sunday. An online opportunity to gather opens doors for new people, and that is key to remember as we look toward the church's future.

---

65 Estes, Douglas (2009), *SimChurch: Being the Church in the Virtual World,* Zondervan, Kindle Edition. Page 231.

66 Chris Ender is Executive Vice-President of Communications at CBS.

67 Cathleen Taff is President, Production Services, Franchise Management, and Multicultural Engagement at the Walt Disney Company.

Cathleen gave me the wisdom that "Not leaning in will be harder for congregations than leaning in." Her words caused me to reflect that, while this can be a real challenge, not doing this work is harder in the long run. If you have found yourself at a church where things were not done ten years ago that today have caused the congregation to struggle, you know how important it is to face our future with eyes open.

So, how will you enter into this digital expedition? Here are the top seven ideas:

1. Know that most everyone today is online in some shape or form, which opens doors for ministry. (Introduction)

2. Embrace the reality that the question isn't should the church be online (it already is), but what kind of online church should it be? (Chapter 1)

3. Know that as you move from the big first step of online worship to online ministry, you can do this by keeping it simple, focusing on engagement, sticking with the basics, and taking next steps. (Chapter 2)

4. Develop an online engagement pathway. Make steps that are easy to see and take. (Chapter 3)

5. Remember that evangelism happens online when we have a plan and take some risks. (Chapter 4)

6. Use engagement as your primary vitality measurement. (Chapter 5)

7. Accept that hybrid ministry isn't coming, it is here, and it is doable. (Chapter 6)

I was excited to write this resource because I know that online ministry changes lives. I have talked with couples who love worship but whose special needs or small children have kept them from attending until a live stream brought worship to their homes. I have laughed with new members who have found hope in Jesus and wanted to commit to him without needing a building to make it real. I have found my own spiritual life blossom as I have done daily prayer with an app and gathered weekly in an online small group.

I am not a tech person by nature. Being born in the 1960's I am not a digital native, but I have found partners, YouTube videos, and tools that have helped me serve a growing congregation and reach new people with God's love.

Welcome to the digital expedition.

What is *The Greatest Expedition*?

The Greatest Expedition is a congregational journey for churches, charges, or cooperative parishes led by a church Expedition Team of 8-12 brave pioneering leaders. The purpose of *The Greatest Expedition* is to provide an experience for Expedition Teams to explore their local context in new ways to develop new MAPS (ministry action plans) so you are more relevant and contextual to reach new people in your community. Updated tools and guides are provided for the church's Expedition Team. Yet, it is a "choose your own adventure" type of journey.

The tools and guides will be provided, but it is up to the church's Expedition Team to decide which tools are needed, which tools just need sharpening, which tools can stay in their backpack to use at a later time, what pathways to explore, and what pathways to pass.

The Greatest Expedition provides a new lens and updated tools to help your Expedition Team explore and think about being the church in different ways. Will your Expedition Team need to clear the overgrown brush from a once known trail, but not recently traveled? Or will the Expedition Team need to cut a brand new trail with their new tools? Or perhaps, will the Team decide they need to move to a completely fresh terrain and begin breaking ground for something brand new in a foreign climate?

Registration is open and Expedition Teams are launching!

greatestexpedition.com

REACH NEW PEOPLE

The Greatest Expedition

GREATESTEXPEDITION.COM

Nineteen leaders you know and trust have been working more than a year to create 23 books, leadership materials, expedition maps, and events for local congregations, districts, conferences and other groups.

SUE NILSON KIBBEY
Breakthrough Prayer

PHIL MAYNARD
Venture Preparation

KAY KOTAN
Assessing the Current Venture

PAUL NIXON
Cultural Competency

OLU BROWN
A New Kind of Venture Leader

KELLY BROWN
Equipping Lay Venture Leaders

JAYE JOHNSON
Expedition Accountability

KEN WILLARD
The What, Why and Where of the New Expedition

KENDA CREASY-DEAN
Expanding the Expedition Through Social Innovation

DAN JACKSON
Generative Leadership

BLAKE BRADFORD
Strengthening Decision-Making and Governance

CHRISTIAN COON
Evangelizing the Christian

JASON MACKEY
Intentional New Relational Building

MILES WELCH
Creating and Sustaining a Prevailing Expedition

DAN PEZET
Community Connection

RACHEL GILMORE
Missional Communities

KEN NASH
Expanding the Expedition through Multi-Sites

WAYNE SCHMIDT
Marketplace Multipliers

NICOLE REILLEY
Expanding the Expedition through Digital Ministry

greatestexpedition.com

Visit us on Facebook at:

facebook.com/GreatestExpedition